A Guide for Taking BeYOUtiful Internal
Selfies to Discover a More Confident YOU

My
Selfie
NEEDS NO
FILTER®

Erica Lanes

My Selfie Needs No Filter

Copyright 2023 © Erica Lanes

Published By Erica Lanes, LLC
P.O. Box 16266
Pensacola, FL 32507
www.EricaLanes.com

Distributed by IngramSpark.

Printed in the United States.

ISBN: 979-8-9880694-0-9

10 9 8 7 6 5 4 3 2

Epigraph

You are AMAZING how you are. More BeYOUtiful
than you can see. STRONGER than you may feel.
More WORTHY than you know. Your Selfie Needs
No Filter. Find Your Lane. Step Into It!

—Erica Lanes

Table of Contents

Dedication Page

This book is dedicated to everyone who attended the 2022 **My Selfie Needs No Filter**: Little Ladies of Leadership Conference. Special resignation is given to the BeYOUtiful ladies listed below who have committed themselves to this international movement and mission. You are phenomenal!

Aaliyah J.	Ailani S.	Ashleigh B.
Breanna J.	Daysia M.	Derielle M.
Dezstani G.	Gabrielle B.	Ivieaeh H.
Jamoria N.	Kaloni G.	Kennede T.
Keonna H.	Maliah C.	Mylah C.
Nia E.	Ollie T.	Racheal M.
Savannah G.	Taneia L.	Zamylah D.

Introduction

Ladies! First thing first: You are unapologetically DOPE, period. What exactly does that mean? That means you are as beautiful on the inside as on the outside. It means you have a special "sauce" no one else has. It's like that secret Mac Sauce from McDonald's that people have tried to duplicate, but can't seem to get it right. That's you. No one on the planet has the unique characteristics, talents, and abilities you do. You can't be copied and then pasted. These things put you in a special lane of your own.

Being in your own lane has many benefits. Yeah, it may feel good to share common interests with others, such as music, sports, food, and fashion. Still, there's something magical about having that one "thing" of your own that's not so common as other young ladies your age. You know, that one thing that really sets you apart from everyone else. Maybe you are considered a track star, master chef, math beast, or eyebrow slayer. Reflecting on the unique things that make you who you are is called taking a "selfie."

I know, you're probably used to the word selfie meaning a picture you take of yourself with your phone. However, when we use selfie throughout this book, we're talking about internal selfies and the things that affect what's on the inside of you, such as self-esteem, self-confidence, self-respect, self-care, and self-love. When the word filter is used in this book, we're not talking about altering a picture image. We're referring to ways to alter, or mask, who you truly are on the inside.

"My Selfie Needs No Filter" is a book designed to help you take BeYOUtiful internal selfies to inspire a more confident YOU. Each selfie chapter leads to the next chapter. By the end of the book, you will possess all the keys necessary to unlock the secret of unfiltered selfies. Anytime you, or someone you know, needs a little "pick me up" on rough days at school, home, or work, thumb through the pages of this book and let it serve as a reminder that you are unapologetically DOPE, and your selfie needs no filter to feel good about yourself or who you are.

My
Selfie
NEEDS NO
FILTER

Chapter One
Oh, S.N.A.P.!

Snapping a few selfies can be fun. They capture many exciting moments and allow you to share them with your family and friends. You need a certain skill level and know how to get those shots just right, though. Have you ever taken a selfie and thought, "Nah, that's not it!" and deleted the picture? I think we all have. Adjusting your camera's focus, striking the right pose, dismissing photobombs, strong battery power, and good lighting will ensure your selfie is a keeper! Did you know you also need a special skill set to take internal selfies?

Each chapter in this book will show you how to take internal selfies using a unique method called S.N.A.P. When life gets you down, and your selfie levels start to drop, take a moment and S.N.A.P. a selfie! When you S.N.A.P. a selfie, it will help you get through the rough moments in your day and ultimately help you build a life of happiness and enjoyment.

The S.N.A.P. Method

The S.N.A.P. Method consists of four steps: 1. Stop, 2. Name, 3. Action, 4. Props.

1. Stop

When you start feeling down, STOP and take a pause from whatever you are doing at the moment. Pausing will help minimize your distractions so you can focus on your feelings. Sometimes, you must turn down the noise in your mind to listen more carefully to your heart. You may also have to distance yourself from certain people or situations to pause appropriately. That's perfectly fine, as long as it's done respectfully.

2. Name

After you stop, NAME the emotion that is making you feel down. When you correctly identify your exact feeling, it becomes easier to let it go. We feel dozens of emotions daily, so pinpointing the correct one will help you overcome your negative feelings. To help you identify your appropriate feelings, I listed a few examples at the end of the chapter. I also left a few blank spaces for you to add your own words.

3. Action

Once you have named your emotion, it's time to take ACTION! Replace your negative feeling by doing something that takes your emotion away or at least makes you feel better. For instance, if music relaxes you when you feel lonely, load your favorite playlist and listen to a few songs. If writing poetry helps when you're sad, pull out your notebook and pen and start writing. Replacing a negative feeling with a positive action helps keep your internal selfie mirror clean.

4. Props

Now that you have taken action, it's time to give yourself some PROPS. Giving yourself props means giving yourself a few "likes," "hearts," or hand claps for the fantastic things you can accomplish. These are the things that outweigh the negative feelings you may have. Giving yourself props means remembering that you're the dopest version of yourself that could ever exist. It means giving yourself a dose of motivation when you need it most. I've added several selfie props at the end of each chapter. Feel free to use them on the days you need a selfie boost. Remember to look in the mirror and give yourself props every day, even on your best days.

Using the S.N.A.P. Method

The S.N.A.P. Method can be used on yourself and shared with others. Teach your family and friends how to S.N.A.P. a selfie when they are feeling down. The best thing about S.N.A.P. is that you can perform it anywhere and anytime. Sitting in a classroom, hair salon, walking in the mall, in the breakroom at work, or while in the heat of an argument, the S.N.A.P. Method will help you immediately shift your mindset from the negative to the positive. As a result, you prevent your selfie levels from getting too low. Even if you can't take the ACTION step at that moment, you can plan to take action as soon as your time allows. Let's get to snap'n!

List of Emotions

Accused	Afraid	Bitter	Betrayed
Cheated	Confused	Defeated	Disappointed
Disrespected	Embarrassed	Empty	Framed
Frustrated	Guilty	Grumpy	Homesick
Hurt	Insulted	Irritated	Jealous
Judged	Limited	Lonely	Miserable
Misunderstood	Neglected	Nervous	Offended
Overwhelmed	Paranoid	Powerless	Pressured
Regret	Rejected	Shame	Shocked
Sorrow	Threatened	Tired	Unappreciated
Unprepared	Vulnerable	Weak	Worried

My Selfie NEEDS NO FILTER

Chapter Two
Adjust Your Lens

Self-Esteem
A confidence and satisfaction in oneself

Simply put, self-esteem is what you think about yourself. It can be described as how you display your inner self to the outside world. Some people think of self-esteem as pride and confidence in your abilities. While this is true, it's a little deeper than that.

Think of self-esteem as your camera lens. Without a lens, you can't properly adjust your focus on the object you're trying to photograph, such as with a selfie. Sometimes, you need to zoom in, zoom out, or rotate. Just like your camera lens allows you to focus on objects, your self-esteem lens allows you to focus on your feelings. Your self-esteem lens must remain clean and scratch-free to help you see past negative thoughts, feelings, and vibes. When your lens becomes dirty, you must find ways to clean it.

There Are Levels to This

Your self-esteem lens can determine if you look at things from a negative or positive viewpoint. It can also decide if you are successful at something or not. Let's say you decide to try out for the basketball or cheerleading team, and your self-esteem lens is dirty. Even though you have all the skills and talent to make the team, you may feel like you don't have what it takes. The result: You bomb tryouts because you let your negative feelings stand in the way of showing off your skills to the judges and coaches.

Your self-esteem is a mighty force that can go up and down. There are three levels to your self-esteem that you should be aware of:

3 Levels of Self-Esteem

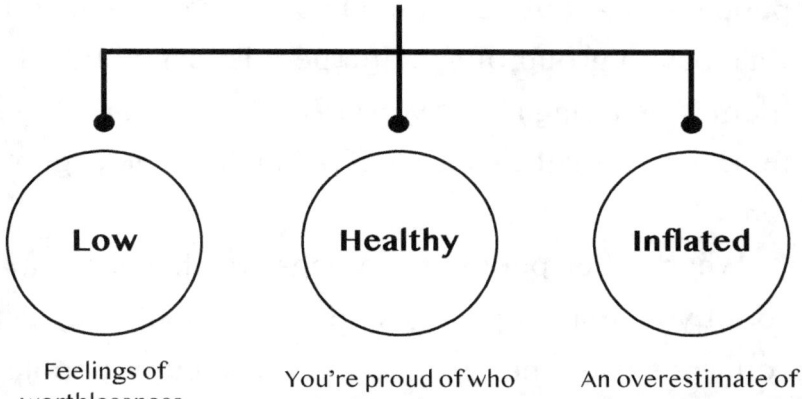

Low	Healthy	Inflated
Feelings of worthlessness. You may not feel proud of who you are.	You're proud of who you are and are not afraid to show up as your true authentic self.	An overestimate of who you are. Your beliefs about yourself are over the top, and you exaggerate yourself.

www.MySelfieNeedsNoFilter.com

12

Not Too Low

Low self-esteem is just how it sounds. It gives you a low, or negative, feeling about yourself. Sometimes, low self-esteem is caused by how other people treat you. Have you ever been bullied? Do people talk about you behind your back? When you walk past a group of specific people, can you hear them whispering about you? How does it make you feel? Do you get upset, cry, or laugh at their ignorance?

When other people have negative things to say about you, many times, it's not even about you; it's your positive energy. It makes insecure people uncomfortable when you show you can think for yourself, dare to be different, and achieve incredible things. They try to take your shine by making you feel bad, but the only thing negative people can take from you are notes on how a brave, BeYOUtiful, and bold young lady carries herself!

If things get too out of hand, don't feel bad about reporting the behavior to the proper people and letting them handle it. In the meantime, when you wake up every morning, look in the mirror and tell yourself you're THAT GIRL and not worried about what H.A.T.E.R.S. say (we'll talk more about H.A.T.E.R.S. a little later).

Way Up

Inflated self-esteem is the opposite of low self-esteem. An inflated self-esteem will make you think you're something or someone you're not. You exaggerate or lie about your abilities, knowledge, or achievements to make yourself look good. A person with inflated self-esteem can be spotted a mile away. They usually get caught in their lies and spend time trying to defend them. People with inflated self-esteem always seem to end their exaggerated stories with something like, "No cap" (no lie) when in reality, they are cap'n!

Healthy Does It!

Healthy self-esteem is the sweet spot. It's where you always want to try to maintain your balance. When you have healthy self-esteem, you are more likely to carry positive vibes. When you don't allow people's negative opinions determine how you feel about yourself, you're displaying healthy self-esteem. You're not concerned with what "they" say about you. If you want to post your selfie, post it for YOU. If you want to get cute and swagged out, do it for YOU. Be happy for YOU. Who are "they" anyway?

Embracing your natural hair, curvy figure, face freckles, or chipped tooth is a sign that you have healthy self-esteem and love what you see in the mirror, but it's not only about loving what you see in your external reflection. It's about loving what you see in your internal reflection as well. It's about loving your beliefs, morals, culture, and personality. It's loving who you are as a person and how you treat other people.

Having this kind of love and respect for yourself screams healthy self-esteem! Let's be clear. Along with having healthy self-esteem and being true to your authentic self, you must be willing to welcome productive feedback, or comments from others. These are opportunities to become an even better version of yourself. Don't become stubborn and develop an "oh well, this is just who I am" attitude. You protect your selfie lens by demonstrating your ability to handle complaints, negative comments, or those sneaky curve balls life throws at you. Knowing how to accept productive feedback from others is a great sign of maturity. It will keep your selfie lens super focused.

Your Front Row

So, what if you have low self-esteem? What can you do? My first piece of advice is to take a look at your "front row." Your front row is reserved for special people only. You're the superstar on the stage of your life's story, and your front row consists of the ones who are front and center enjoying the show.

Your front row is supporters who will clap and cheer for you. They are there to lift you up, not tear you down. They will make you feel good about who you are and what you stand for. Even if you don't see your front row face-to-face all the time, you will always feel them heart-to-heart wherever you are.

Your front row will also include people who will tell you "no," challenge you, and let you know when you're wrong. You want people like this on your front row because they will keep it 100 with you. They want the best for you and will lovingly tell you things that may be hard to hear. Their goal is to help you become a better version of yourself, so you can continue to give a fantastic performance.

People who are not on your front row should only watch your show from a far distance. These are negative people who bring you down. Try spending as less time with them as possible. Negative people, and negative energy, are like fire extinguishers. They're designed to kill your star fire. Don't let them.

Protect your peace by creating a positive energy zone. Set up emotional barriers for those you allow on your front row and those you don't. People with negative energy should remain on the back row, and people with positive energy are welcome to sit up front and enjoy the show. Who's on your front row? What does it look like? What does it sound like?

It's wise to evaluate your front row from time to time. You want to make sure negative people don't try to sneak on. You also want to make sure that positive people don't turn into negative people. If they do, offer them a seat on the back row or, better yet, out the door!

Are you sitting in someone else's front row? Are

you a supporter of someone you care about? If not, find someone who deserves your support and attention, and give it to them. Enjoy cheering them on and clapping for them from their front row. Doing so is a huge self-esteem booster, not for them but for you!

Research shows that supporting others and doing nice things for them helps improve your self-esteem levels. Support those you care about from their front row. They're the superstar of their life story, and you're the superstar of yours. They will clap for you, and you will clap for them.

It's healthy to celebrate other people's successes and accomplishments. There's no room for jealousy or envy when you both are shining stars. The world actually needs more stars. The sky would be pretty dark with only one shining star in it.

Spread a Little Kindness

Doing kind things for people in places where you learn, play, pray, and work are other great self-esteem boosters. Make it a point to do something for others that will make you proud of being the kindhearted person you are. No good deed is too small to make a difference. Below are examples of kind things you can do to brighten someone's day while boosting your self-esteem levels.

www.MySelfieNeedsNoFilter.com

Sometimes, we can be our worst critics, but don't be so hard on yourself. While mistakes are a part of life, they don't define who you are. Failures will also happen, but failing proves you're at least trying. If you're starting to tear yourself down, stop and think about what you would tell a friend if your current problem were theirs. What piece of advice would you give them? How would you make them feel better about themselves? Show yourself some kindness and consider taking your own advice from time to time. It would help to ask yourself the following questions:

- What happened?

- What factors influenced this decision?

- What have I learned from this experience?

- What are my plans to move in a positive

  direction?

- What are three things I do really well?

Planted, Not Buried

There may come a time when the darkness becomes very heavy. You may struggle to find your place in the world while searching for your true identity. Your self-esteem decreases, and you feel nothing is working out for you. You feel like your struggles are burying you deeper and deeper into the ground. Don't ever give up hope.

Understand that you have not been buried by life's struggles, but have been planted in new soil designed to birth a stronger version of you. This version will prove stronger, wiser, and more victorious than ever. Keep your selfie lens focused, cleaned, and free from cracks. Get ready to take BeYOUtiful selfies. It's time to strike a pose!

S.N.A.P. a Selfie!
Self-Esteem

List five things you do to boost
your self-esteem levels.

1. _____

2. _____

3. _____

4. _____

5. _____

What makes you feel good about yourself?

_____

_____

_____

_____

_____

SELF-ESTEEM
PROPS

SELF-ESTEEM
PROPS

" I am so
much more
than what I
see in
the mirror. "

www.MySelfieNeedsNoFilter.com

SELF-ESTEEM
✦
PROPS

" I do not need to
be perfect. I just
need to be true
to myself. "

www.MySelfieNeedsNoFilter.com

SELF-ESTEEM
❖
PROPS

" I must be happy
with my off-line
life as well as
my on-line life **"**

www.MySelfieNeedsNoFilter.com

SELF-ESTEEM
PROPS

" I am loyal, ambitious, and beautiful. Anyone who does not see that does not deserve me. "

www.MySelfieNeedsNoFilter.com

SELF-ESTEEM
PROPS

My H.A.T.E.R.S.
are my biggest
motivators

www.MySelfieNeedsNoFilter.com

SELF-ESTEEM
PROPS

Note to Self:
I am amazing
I am capable
I am strong
I am fierce

www.MySelfieNeedsNoFilter.com

SELF-ESTEEM
✤
PROPS

❝

What I think of me
is more important
than what foolish
people think of me

❞

www.MySelfieNeedsNoFilter.com

SELF-ESTEEM
PROPS

I am like the
sun. I just
keep shining.

www.MySelfieNeedsNoFilter.com

SELF-ESTEEM
PROPS

> I am proud of
> the woman
> I am becoming

www.MySelfieNeedsNoFilter.com

SELF-ESTEEM
PROPS

My mistakes do
not define who I
am

www.MySelfieNeedsNoFilter.com

My Selfie

NEEDS NO FILTER

Chapter Three
Strike a Pose

Self-Confidence
Confidence in oneself and in one's
powers and abilities

Simply put, self-confidence is how you feel about your ability to do certain things. Self-confidence is like striking a pose for a selfie. When you strike a pose, you may keep your chin up, stick your chest out, and stand tall. Likewise, a person with healthy self-confidence displays these same traits daily.

Do you remember hearing about that unforgettable moment in pop culture when Kanye West stormed the stage and interrupted Taylor Swift as she tried to accept the 2009 MTV VMA for Best Video by a Female Artist? You may have witnessed the event firsthand or seen a video clip. If not, look it up! In front of thousands of people in the audience and viewers watching from home, Taylor stood mortified as Kanye grabbed her microphone and told her how undeserving she was of the honor. Although Kanye later apologized to Taylor (fist bump to Kanye), she spent years trying to overcome the shame, hurt, and embarrassment. Her confidence level dropped.

H. A. T. E. R. S.

The situation with Kayne and Taylor serves as a reminder that no matter how successful and on top of your game you are, there will always be H.A.T.E.R.S. of your craft and talent. H.A.T.E.R.S. means:

- **H**aving
- **A**nger
- **T**owards
- **E**veryone
- **R**eaching
- **S**uccess

H.A.T.E.R.S. don't like seeing other people shine and will try to make them look bad or discredit their ability. Displaying confidence and remembering you're THAT GIRL will help you overcome situations like this. Your brain is like a garden. It will grow what you plant. If you plant positive thoughts, it will produce positive energy. Likewise, if you plant negative thoughts and opinions of H.A.T.E.R.S., it will produce negative energy. The best part of all is you're in control. You decide if you're planting flowers or weeds. What will your garden grow?

Confidence "Cape-of-Abilities"

Having good self-confidence helps you build self-trust and gives you courage. Have you ever heard that little voice in your mind say, "You're not smart enough, popular enough, or have what it takes"? Why do we listen to that part of our brain? Sometimes it's caused by allowing other people's opinions to get trapped in our heads. Other times it's because we underestimate our abilities. Most of the time, it's caused by fear. When the effects of fear start to overpower your confidence, remember these three letters, W.T.F.: Welcome the Fear.

When it's time to W.T.F., pull out your Confidence Cape. Have you ever avoided new challenges or trying new things because of the fear of failing? Imagine your Confidence Cape as an invisible cape that blocks all fear and doubt from entering your mind. This cape gives you the power to swoop down and go head-to-head with any challenge. As long as you have on this cape, your abilities are endless. Your Confidence Cape is your secret weapon for all "cape-of-abilities."

Confident, Not Cocky

Confidence is very different from being cocky. Have you ever met a cocky person? They usually brag about their accomplishments and come off as being conceited or arrogant. You may know her by her first name, "Miss-Know-It-All." They often blame others for their mistakes because they're a "perfect 10," right? Wrong!

A cocky person is full of filters. They overemphasize their abilities to try to be something they're not. They're almost like a person with inflated self-esteem, except a cocky person will try to make other people look bad so they look good. This is not how you remain true to yourself and display confidence. Confidence is being honest about your abilities, talents, and knowledge and owning all of it, even if you fail while doing it. It's great to be proud of your accomplishments and share them with your supporters. This is not being cocky. Real supporters will be proud and clap for you. H.A.T.E.R.S., however, will think you're being cocky and say you're doing too much. Those people are not your supporters. Know the difference between your H.A.T.E.R.S. and your supporters.

Let's Get Social

What's your favorite social media platform? Is it Instagram, TikTok, Snapchat, YouTube, or Facebook? Whatever it is, I'm sure you find it entertaining and packed with the latest styles, fashion, celebrity news, and dance challenges. It's where you like interacting with friends, posting selfies, and passing the time away. This is great, but you must be careful.

Social media can change your entire mood and alter how you feel about yourself. It has placed unrealistic standards of what being beautiful, popular, and accepted truly means. This has caused people to compare themselves to what they see on the screen and set unreachable goals. This has decreased self-confidence and self-esteem for many people, including adults.

Have you ever posted something on social media that you thought was so good you knew at least 1,000 people would like, share, or comment on your post? Instead, you may have only received two engagements, you and your bestie. Or, maybe you've seen posts and pictures from friends spending time together and hanging out, but you weren't invited. Has either of these examples made you feel a little down, perhaps even like you were being left out? If so, you're not alone.

Research says depression, anxiety, loneliness, and FoMO (Fear of Missing Out) are connected to social media. Seeing how pretty, talented, and creative some social media influencers are may make you question your beauty. You may feel like you don't have what it takes to be accepted and popular like them. Their posts rack up thousands of "likes." Everyone raves about their greatness while you barely get noticed. Here's a little secret about social media. You can't believe everything you see and hear. It's full of filters.

Sometimes, the influencers you follow actually pay people to follow them and engage with their posts. Their faces and bodies are so heavily filtered you probably wouldn't recognize them if you saw them in person. The adventurous places they go, expensive things they buy, and famous friends they claim to have are lies, fake, or exaggerated. Do yourself a favor, and don't believe the hype! Be careful about the people you follow on social media. Their bad behavior and lifestyle will rub off on you and turn you into a person with low selfie levels. Follow the ones who make you want to step your game up and become a better version of yourself.

A Little Boost

Check out the following tips if you're looking to boost your self-confidence. Feel free to add your suggestions to the list:

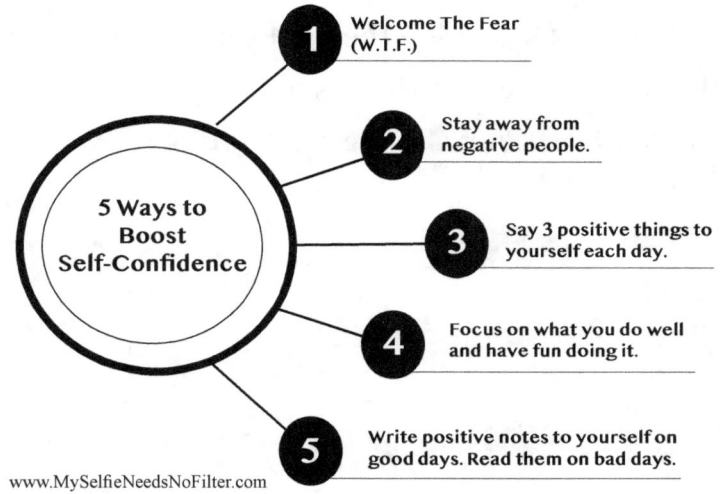

1. Welcome The Fear (W.T.F.)
2. Stay away from negative people.
3. Say 3 positive things to yourself each day.
4. Focus on what you do well and have fun doing it.
5. Write positive notes to yourself on good days. Read them on bad days.

5 Ways to Boost Self-Confidence

www.MySelfieNeedsNoFilter.com

Keep Shining

When people close the doors of opportunity on you, cut the lights off on your creativity, and try to put your value on "clearance," your self-confidence and self-esteem levels may drop. However, there's one thing about you... You don't quit! How do I know? Because you're still here. You've survived 100% of all the struggles life has thrown you so far.

When negative people try to sprinkle negative vibes on you, dust your shoulders off, hold your head high, and give them a big smile. Because, no matter what they try to do or say, you will never quit. Soon, all your H.A.T.E.R.S. will see the light that shines brightly within you and realize there's nothing they can do to stop your fire. Keep shining. I'm rooting for you!

S.N.A.P. a Selfie!
Self-Confidence

List five things you do to boost your self-confidence
levels. What are your star "cape-of-abilities"
(things you do really well)?

1. _____

2. _____

3. _____

4. _____

5. _____

SELF-CONFIDENCE
PROPS

SELF-CONFIDENCE
PROPS

66

I glow differently when my
confidence is fueled by belief in
myself instead of
validation from others

SELF-CONFIDENCE
PROPS

66

Confidence is about
walking into a room and not
needing to compare
myself to anyone else

www.MySelfieNeedsNoFilter.com

47

SELF-CONFIDENCE
PROPS

66

I
GROW
through what I
GO
through

www.MySelfieNeedsNoFilter.com

SELF-CONFIDENCE
PROPS

66

Sometimes I'm
BEAUTY
and the
BEAST

www.MySelfieNeedsNoFilter.com

SELF-CONFIDENCE
PROPS

66

The only person
I should ever
compare myself to is
who I used to be

SELF-CONFIDENCE
PROPS

66

Life is
tough
but so
am I

www.MySelfieNeedsNoFilter.com

66

I am two things:
WHO
and
WHAT
I want to be

www.MySelfieNeedsNoFilter.com

SELF-CONFIDENCE
✥
PROPS

66

I won't let
people talk fear
into my goals.
Move out my way!

SELF-CONFIDENCE
✤
PROPS

66

I will be so positive
that negative people
follow me on social media

www.MySelfieNeedsNoFilter.com

SELF-CONFIDENCE
✤
PROPS

66

What I'm not
going to do
is give up on myself

www.MySelfieNeedsNoFilter.com

My Selfie NEEDS NO FILTER

Chapter Four
Photobomb

Self-Respect
A proper respect for oneself as a human being

To truly understand self-respect, it's important to understand what respect generally means. The first time the word respect got my full attention was when I heard the legendary soul singer, Aretha Franklin, sing about it in her number one hit song, Respect. The way she blares out the spelling R.E.S.P.E.C.T., it's no wonder the song became a national anthem for female empowerment. The song was, and still is, a demand from confident and independent women worldwide to be treated with value and appreciation.

More Than Enough

Showing respect to others has less to do with

their character and more to do with the reflection of your character as a good person. Whether they're the C.E.O., school teacher, or janitor, you must still show them respect. Showing respect means giving space to allow people to be authentic and accepting them doing their own thing and thinking their own thoughts. It doesn't mean you have to agree with them. It means you understand that people have feelings that do not always have to align with yours.

Do you get irritated when a friend or family member tries to give you advice? Even if they're dead wrong about something, take a moment and allow them to have their opinion. I am willing to bet they have provided you with other pieces of valuable advice at some point along the way. Let them have their thoughts without being so salty. It's a sign of respect and pays off in the long run.

Self-respect means being proud of who you are. It's about treating yourself how you want others to treat you. To do this, it starts with you recognizing your self-worth. It takes a lot of courage to be authentic, especially in a world that constantly tells you who you should be. The world may even try to convince you that you're not good enough, but I'm here to tell you that you are more than enough and have always been enough.

Messy Messes

You were created with the sugar, spice, and everything nice to be a girl on fire! You're here to shine and blaze the world with your special sauce and uniqueness. However, when you surround yourself with messy people, who spread messy rumors and like to start messes, it will make you feel worthless. You no longer feel proud of yourself, and your self-respect levels will fall. To make your levels rise again, surround yourself with positive people who don't like to get dirty with other people's messes.

Self-respect is the most powerful gift you can give yourself. Don't allow anyone to steal your gift away. Be brave enough to stand up for what's right without apologizing. Starting today, I want you to believe, deep down in your soul, that everyone who comes in contact with you is in contact with someone who has value and deserves R.E.S.P.E.C.T. because you are more than enough. Read that last sentence again, this time out loud.

Flag on the Play

Now, let's get real about self-respect for a moment. Sex-ting, sleeping around, using drugs, smoking, vaping, and underage drinking are NOT it. If you want people to respect you and not treat you like a used tampon, you must know how to stand up for yourself and say, "No, thank you, I'm good." This rings self-respect loud and clear.

It's important to recognize red flags (warning signs), to avoid disrespect from others. Here are a few to think about:

- If your friend always asks to copy your homework or only wants to sit by you in class on test days so they can copy your answers, this is a red flag.

- If your bae only wants to come to your house when no one else is home, so you two can be alone, this is a red flag.

- If your friends only text or call on your paydays and ask to borrow money, this is a red flag.

- If someone is waving red flags on things that make you uncomfortable, it's time to S.N.A.P. a selfie. Find time to talk with them about how their actions make you feel. This sends the message that you're a person with high levels of self-respect and demand respect from them too.

Not allowing people to use or mistreat you is the grandest form of self-respect. It's like being on the lookout for an annoying photobomb. Have you ever tried to take a selfie, and someone jumps in your background as a prank to spoil your picture? You spend time getting your focus just right and finding the perfect pose, then here comes someone, or something, trying to ruin your photo. Sometimes it's funny, but other times it can be so aggy. Practicing self-respect is like not allowing a photobomb to invade your space, intentions, or goals.

"No" is a Complete Sentence

You must learn to say "no" to certain things (no is a complete sentence, B.T.W.). People who don't respect your "no" don't deserve a "yes" either. You may find it hard to say no. Keep in mind, "no" does not have to mean "not at all"; it may just mean "not right now." If you have a hard time telling people no, below are a few ways that may be a little more comfortable for you:

- I wish there were two of me, but I can't.
- I'm sorry, but not this time.
- It sounds like fun! But I have another commitment that day.
- Thank you for the invitation! Please think of me next time.
- Thank you for thinking of me, but I can't this time.
- It's a NO for Me.

Saying no and resisting peer pressure can be a challenge. Ask yourself the following questions to help you make your final decisions. Here's a tip: DON'T DO IT if your answers could lead to trouble or disappointment!

- What kind of person do I want to be known as, for

myself and for the ones who look up to me?
- What do my morals say about me?
- Is it really worth it?
- What are the consequences of my choices? Could I end up:
    o Arrested
    o Pregnant
    o Fired from my job
    o Kicked out of school
    o Disappointing my loved ones
    o Contracting an S.T.D. (Sexually Transmitted Disease)?
    o ALL OF THE ABOVE?!

Badge of Honor

When you start to feel disrespected by other people or circumstances, it may be your cue to exit stage left. Have you ever watched a reality T.V. show where people argue, fight, and put each other down all the time while saying things like, "I don't do drama"? Ironically, the people who say this usually cause the most drama throughout the episode. Not only do they lack respect for the other cast members, but they also lack self-respect. If you are face to face with people like this, let them have their drama while you move to the left. It's a great way of displaying your self-respect like a badge of honor.

Wear your self-respect badge of honor with pride for all to see. Make sure it shines so brightly that everyone knows you're someone who understands your worth and demands R.E.S.P.E.C.T. They must know you're here to play zero games about it. You can't force anyone to respect you, but you can refuse to be disrespected.

Remember this: self-respect is at the heart of who you truly are. It is a measure of your character, self-worth, and values. Self-respect is the foundation for self-love and demands appreciation from you. Don't allow a photobomb to ruin your selfie. After so many selfie attempts, you will need to eventually recharge your battery.

S.N.A.P. a Selfie!
Self-Respect

List five things you do to boost your
self-respect level. What makes
you proud of yourself?

1. _____

2. _____

3. _____

4. _____

5. _____

SELF-RESPECT
PROPS

SELF-RESPECT
✣
PRÓPS

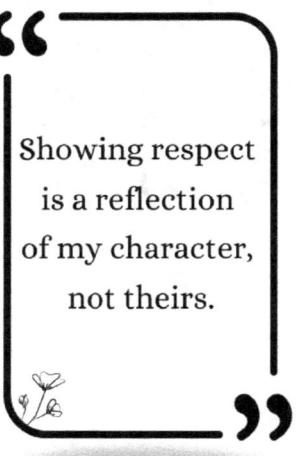

> Showing respect
> is a reflection
> of my character,
> not theirs.

www.MySelfieNeedsNoFilter.com

SELF-RESPECT
✤
PROPS

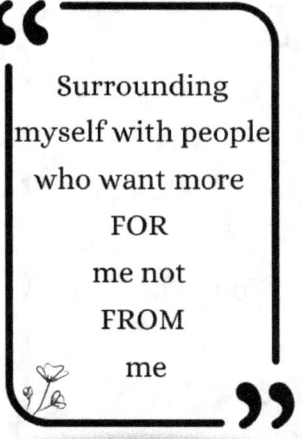

> Surrounding
> myself with people
> who want more
> FOR
> me not
> FROM
> me

www.MySelfieNeedsNoFilter.com

SELF-RESPECT
PROPS

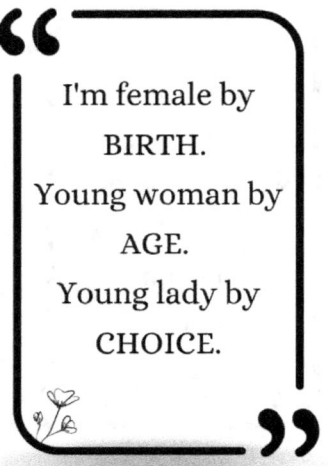

> I'm female by
> BIRTH.
> Young woman by
> AGE.
> Young lady by
> CHOICE.

www.MySelfieNeedsNoFilter.com

SELF-RESPECT
PROPS

" Self Respect

+

Self Love

=

New Lifestyle "

www.MySelfieNeedsNoFilter.com

SELF-RESPECT
✤
PRÖPS

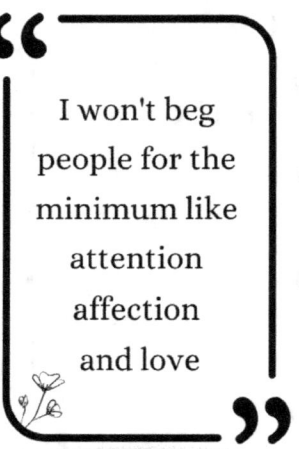

" I won't beg
people for the
minimum like
attention
affection
and love "

www.MySelfieNeedsNoFilter.com

SELF-RESPECT
PROPS

I know my
WORTH
and I'm adding
TAX!

www.MySelfieNeedsNoFilter.com

SELF-RESPECT
PROPS

If I'm treated
like a joke
I'll leave like it is
funny

www.MySelfieNeedsNoFilter.com

73

SELF-RESPECT
PROPS

"
I will not ever
let anyone
save me
for later
"

SELF-RESPECT
✤
PROPS

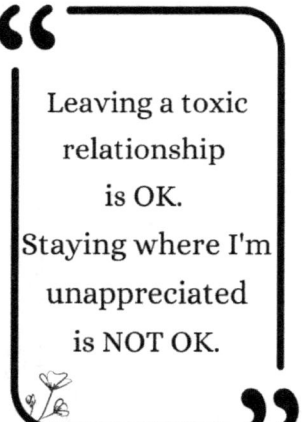

> Leaving a toxic
> relationship
> is OK.
> Staying where I'm
> unappreciated
> is NOT OK.

www.MySelfieNeedsNoFilter.com

SELF-RESPECT
✤
PROPS

> I will not let anyone treat me like I'm regular glue. I'm GLITTER GLUE.

My Selfie
NEEDS NO FILTER

Chapter Five

Recharge Your Battery

Self-Care
Care for oneself

When you hear the word self-care, personal hygiene probably pops in your mind. Several things equal self-care, but let's start there first. Personal hygiene, the things you do to keep the outside of your body clean and healthy, is very important in preventing body odor, acne outbreaks, infections, rashes, and rotten teeth. As a young lady, you must ensure your hygiene is on point. Here are a few tips on making sure your hygiene is always top-tier:

PERSONAL HYGIENE TIPS!

Take Frequent Showers

Use Deodorant

Cleanse Your Face

Wear Clean Clothes and Underwear

Change Your Sanitary Pads

Brush and Floss Your Teeth

Keep Your Nails Clean

Wash Your Hair

Wipe from Front to Back

www.MySelfieNeedsNoFilter.com

From the Inside Out

We can't talk about taking care of the outside of your body if we don't talk about taking care of the inside. When you think about being healthy, you may think about your diet and what you put in your body. However, your diet is not only what you physically eat. It's what you watch, listen to, read, the company you keep, and your thoughts. You must take care of this part of your diet. Consuming too much "fat" (negativity) will cause you to gain unwanted weight.

Your body is designed to tell you what it needs. When your stomach growls, you may be hungry. When your mouth is dry, you may be thirsty. When you yawn, you may be sleepy. Listening to your body and caring for your needs is extremely important and part of self-care. If you don't, it could lead to damaging effects. You may need to power up to remain healthy from the inside out.

Time to Reset

Let's look a little deeper into self-care. Have you ever felt like this, "I am tired, frustrated, and irritated! I have only one nerve left, and everyone at school, home, work, and this team is dancing on it! I just want to scream and make everyone disappear!" You may need a mental reset if so.

Resetting is a way of pausing your routine and recharging your battery or energy. It's a way to give something else your attention for a while. It allows you to clear your mind and chill out. Resetting is like restarting your phone: bad vibes (bad data) are removed, your thoughts (unnecessary running apps) are cleared, and your energy (performance) is better. Resetting is also a part of self-care.

Headaches, stomach aches, tightness in your chest, and difficulty breathing are clues your body needs to reset. It could mean you're overwhelmed or stressed. Be sure to seek medical attention immediately if you feel these things are getting worse or have occurred over time.

Participating in activities that you enjoy can help you get through tough times. These activities make you feel good and should be built into your weekly routine. Practicing this type of self-care, even if only for 10mins, can help you develop a more positive mindset and give others, and yourself, a better version of yourself.

Below are a few examples of mental reset activities you may want to try:

Take a Nap

Meditate

Pray

Listen to Music

Get a Massage

Excercise

Read/Listen to a Book

Avoid Drugs, Smoking and Alcohol

Time to Reset Activties

www.MySelfieNeedsNoFilter.com

I love visiting my "Think Tank" when it's time for a mental reset. A Think Tank is where you can be alone to just... think! It may be in your room, the shower, your car, or the "porcelain throne" (the toilet). When you take a few moments to visit your Think Tank, it provides peace and quiet to rest and reflect on your day. I encourage you to visit your Think Tank often.

Make Your Bed

What is one of the first things you do when you get up in the morning? I bet one thing is grabbing your cell phone to check your messages or social media accounts! A typical morning self-care routine could look like this: use the bathroom, wash your face, brush your teeth, get dressed, feed your pet, eat breakfast, and out the door you go. While this is a standard routine, there's an important step missing. Make your bed.

You may feel that making your bed wastes time because you will hop back in when you return home anyway. Although this may be true, did you know this simple step can equal great success? Being mindful about making your bed in the morning helps you become mindful about other things you do through-out the day, such as daily chores, important meet-ings, and commitments you've made to others. Building productive habits like this into your morn-ing routine will trickle over to other aspects of your life and help keep you in your lane for success.

If making your bed is your first task, even before eating breakfast, it will help jump-start your day on the right foot. It will put you in a good mood and bring you positive vibes. Research shows that people with mental health conditions are usually happier when their homes and rooms are clean. A clean external environment can provide a sense of peace for the internal environment located in your brain. As you can see, making your bed is a simple and great way to practice self-care.

There's nothing like coming home to a freshly made bed after a long day at school, work, or practice. It's a warm invitation to a better night's sleep. Not to mention, it just makes your room look cleaner too. The five minutes it takes to make your bed each day can significantly affect how the rest of your day will flow. It will give you a sense of pride and motivate you to take care of other essential tasks throughout the day. Go make your bed now!

Battery Check

Remember to check your mental, physical, emotional, and spiritual battery life every day. Do you need to power up? If so, it's time for a recharge. Engage in things that will fuel you and give you purpose. Once you've done this, it's lights, camera, action!

S.N.A.P. a Selfie!
Self-Care

List five things you do to practice self-care.
What are things that help you relax?

1. _____

2. _____

3. _____

4. _____

5. _____

SELF-CARE
PROPS

SELF-CARE
PROPS

I will NOT let
other people's
messes get
me dirty

66

www.MySelfieNeedsNoFilter.com

SELF-CARE
❖
PROPS

Note to Self:
I cannot
pour from
an empty cup

66

www.MySelfieNeedsNoFilter.com

SELF-CARE
✧
PROPS

I promise to take
good care of this
version of myself.
I've worked too
hard to let her
down now.

66

SELF-CARE
✣
PROPS

If I need to, I'll
unplug from
everything,
including myself.

66

www.MySelfieNeedsNoFilter.com

91

SELF-CARE

PROPS

My beauty
is an amazing
side effect
of good
self-care

66

www.MySelfieNeedsNoFilter.com

SELF-CARE
PROPS

No longer

I WISH

Only

I WILL

www.MySelfieNeedsNoFilter.com

SELF-CARE
PROPS

Sometimes
self-care looks like
staying home, being
in my own zone,
and telling people
NO

66

www.MySelfieNeedsNoFilter.com

SELF-CARE
PROPS

When Overwhelmed
Remember:
One step at a time
One day at a time
One task at a time
One thought at a time

www.MySelfieNeedsNoFilter.com

SELF-CARE
PROPS

I'll only surround
myself with those who
PRAY
behind my back, not
TALK
behind my back

66

www.MySelfieNeedsNoFilter.com

SELF-CARE
PROPS

If it costs me my
peace, it's too
expensive

My Selfie NEEDS NO FILTER

Chapter Six

Lights, Camera, Action!

Self-Love

Love of self: such as an appreciation of one's own worth or virtue

---

Practicing self-love is showing yourself that you appreciate and value who you are. Close your eyes. Now think about someone you love to the moon and back. It may be your parents, grandparents, siblings, cousins, best friend, or bae. Now, think about how you show love to that person. Do you speak to them with kindness, support them, spend time with them, and speak positivity in their lives? Do you love them for who they are and would do anything for them? Of course, you would! You deserve the same treatment from you as well. When you practice these loving things for yourself, you are practicing self-love.

Let Your Light Shine

When you love yourself, your light shines from the inside out. Self-love is the highest level of feeling that attracts everything you desire. Have you ever heard a movie director yell, "Lights, camera, action!" before they start filming? When you hear this phrase, it means it's show time. Practicing self-love is like saying, "Lights, camera, action!" to yourself. You take action and show yourself kindness and gratitude for being the amazing person you are. Displaying self-love acknowledges that your light shines bright and deserves your appreciation.

A Special Gift

Loving yourself may sound odd to you. You may think love is something you only give to others. But, when you love yourself, you give yourself an extraordinary gift. When you love yourself, it's the secret to your everlasting happiness. You ignite a self-love cycle that will remain with you for a lifetime. Even when people come and go, in and out of your life, your gift of self-love will stand the test of time. It has no expiration date and will always be there when needed. It will not disappoint.

To practice self-love, you must first learn to like yourself. Liking yourselves means you're happy with who you are on the inside and outside. You're pleased with who you are and who you are becoming. Liking yourself will help convince your heart that you are worthy of love. Loving yourself is much deeper. It means you have strong affection and personal attachment to yourself. It's the foundation for all the selfies, so we've saved it for last.

It may take time to reach the level of self-love, but you must get there. Soon, you will start attracting people who show you the same level of love you give yourself. You become a magnet for respect and appreciation when you display your worth to others. It all starts with you showing yourself love and admiration for who you are on the inside.

Love the Skin, You're In

Part of self-love is loving what you see in the mirror. When I was younger, I remember other kids making fun of my big nose, lips, and glasses. The boys used to make fun of my flat chest and say my face looked like a Star Crunch Cookie because of my severe acne; ouch! Every day, there was something new they would pick on me about. My younger brother didn't make it any better. He would always remind me of how big my forehead was. He would say, "go head, forehead!" I remember looking at myself in the mirror and hating what I saw. I had a negative body image.

Body image is how you feel about your body and physical appearance. It's the picture of your body in your mind and how it matches your physical body. You may feel unhappy about your body type and want to change it. You may want to set healthy body goals to make yourself look and feel better, and that's OK. What's not OK is allowing someone else's opinion of your appearance make you hate what you see in the mirror.

Healthy food choices, exercising, taking vitamins, and visiting your doctor are great ways to help you feel better and look better. The critical thing to remember is, unless it's a health risk, make these changes for yourself, not to meet someone else's satisfaction. Don't listen to negative comments about your body from anyone. Your body is not the problem. The problem is their inability to see your authentic beauty. They are blinded by what society views as beautiful and can't see the natural beauty beyond your skin. Love your body for all its uniqueness on the inside and outside. There's nothing more beautiful than being unafraid of being BeYOUtifully, YOU.

While going through my negative body image stage, one person always reminded me of just how beautiful I was, my Grandma Sara. She made me appreciate how my unique features made me special. Her loving words gave me an extra self-esteem boost when I needed it the most. Remember that special sauce we talked about in the introduction? Well, I developed a lot of it, and I'm sure you will too. Whether you're tall, short, curvy, slim, have freckles, or have a chipped tooth, I'm here to tell you, you are unapologetically DOPE and dripping with special sauce!

Take Out the Trash

In my city, Wednesday is usually trash day. That's when a big garbage truck comes through and picks up all the trash you have collected for the week. Everything you want to throw away goes in your trash can, and the garbage truck takes it to the garbage dump. In addition to your physical trash, practice getting rid of your mental and emotional trash. It weighs you down and takes time away from you showing yourself some much needed love. Ask yourself the following five questions to see if you are saving internal trash or treasure:

1.
How can I love myself more each day?

2.
What are 3 negative mindsets I need to change?

3.
When am I the happiest version of myself?

4.
What are 5 things I love about myself?

5.
What do I love about my life?

Reflection
SELF-LOVE
Questions

www.MySelfieNeedsNoFilter.com

Step Into Your Lane

One way to build your self-love is to stop comparing yourself to others. Before taking a test, do you recall your teacher saying, "Keep your eyes on your paper"? The teacher needed to know if your paper was your original work and not copied work of someone else. Take these same guided principles from outside the classroom into the real world. Understand that everyone's journey is different, so you must find your own lane. You may think it's better to "lay your eyes on someone else's paper," but their formula for success is different from yours. You can't use their calculator on your spelling test anyway.

Every moment you spend comparing your life to the lives of others is the time taken away from focusing on your goals. There is a flip side to this. Let's say there's someone you look up to. They're a great role model and are incredibly talented and brilliant. You watch them in action and study their road to success. This may prompt you to make necessary changes to improve so you can level up. This is healthy.

What's unhealthy is wasting time competing with someone else's life. You watch them in action and study their road to success to be better than them. You're always looking for an opportunity to outshine them and will do so at any cost. This mindset needs to be adjusted quickly.

When you compete with others, you put yourself down when you can't measure up to their abilities. You'll start planting negative seeds in your mind and believing you don't have what it takes to be successful. Soon, your selfie levels will drop. Start planting positive seeds instead and watch your garden grow. Understand there's no competition when you're in your own success lane. It was created especially for you and no one else. Step into it!

You Deserve It!

There's no need to flex for others by exaggerating who you truly are. Love your journey with all its twists, turns, and bumps. Life can be so complex yet so simple. Living by golden moral standards, taking care of your body, and loving yourself from the inside out, are the secrets to living well and longer..

Do you recall that list of people you love at the beginning of the chapter? Did your name make that list at first? If not, it's OK. Remember to include your-self when you think about the people you love. You deserve to be loved by you.

Although your life may be colored with the mis-takes, messes, and fires you've made, those are the things that make you who you are. You may have been down but not out. You may have paused but didn't quit. Show yourself some love for being strong, brave, and resilient. Today is perfect for congratulat-ing yourself on how far you've come!

Sweet as Sugar

Giving respect to your body is another form of self-love. Your body is a priceless treasure. It can't be given away to just anyone. Imagine if you had a hand full of sugar. The sugar represents your body and your love. If you keep giving your sugar away, especially to people who don't appreciate you, you won't have any sug-ar left for someone deserving of your love. Hold on tight to your precious sugar. It's more valuable than all the riches in the world.

If you find yourself in a situation where your sugar is unappreciated, it may be time to move on. Move on from toxicity and put your self-esteem, self-confidence, self-respect, and self-care at the forefront. It demonstrates the high level of self-love that you have. You must love and respect yourself to genuinely love and respect others. It starts with believing that your selfie needs no filter and you are worthy of appreciation. Once you reach this level of love, it's time to upload your selfies.

S.N.A.P. a Selfie!
Self-Love

List five things you do to practice self-love.
What are things you do to show appreciation
for yourself?

1. _____

2. _____

3. _____

4. _____

5. _____

SELF-LOVE
PROPS

SELF-LOVE
❖
PROPS

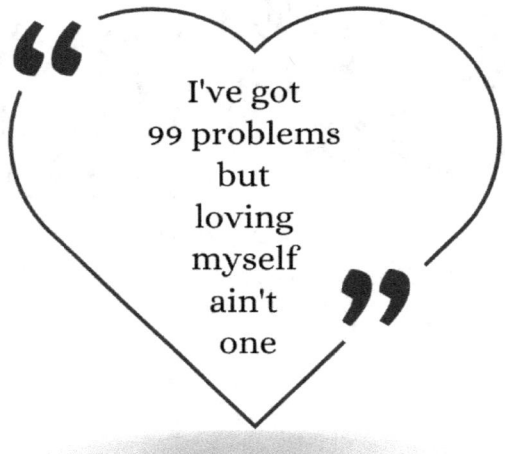

I've got
99 problems
but
loving
myself
ain't
one

www.MySelfieNeedsNoFilter.com

SELF-LOVE
PROPS

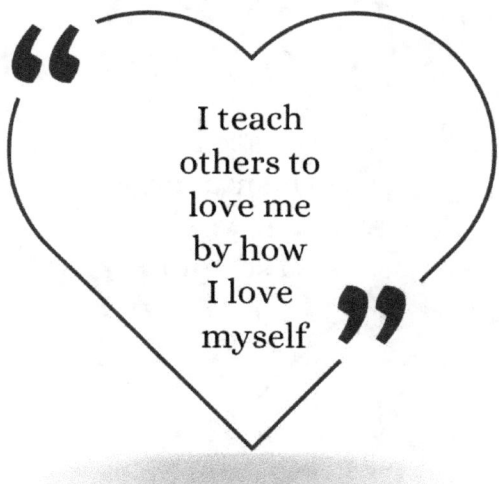

I teach
others to
love me
by how
I love
myself

www.MySelfieNeedsNoFilter.com

SELF-LOVE
✧
PROPS

"
I love what
I see in
the mirror.
I'm worth
a second
look.
"

www.MySelfieNeedsNoFilter.com

SELF-LOVE
❖
PROPS

> Other people
> loving me
> is a bonus.
> ME loving ME
> is the
> real prize.

www.MySelfieNeedsNoFilter.com

SELF-LOVE
✤
PROPS

I am
unapologetically
focused on my
GOALS
GRIND
and
GLOW UP

www.MySelfieNeedsNoFilter.com

SELF-LOVE
✤
PROPS

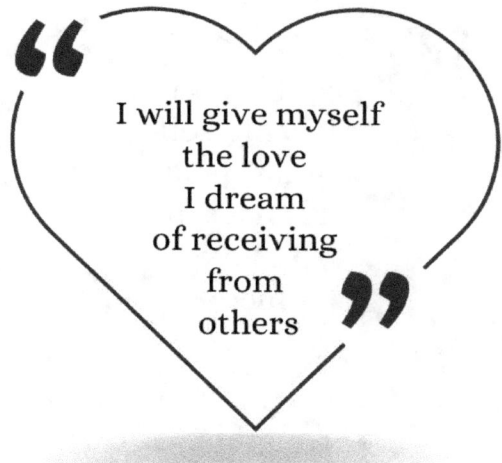

"
I will give myself
the love
I dream
of receiving
from
others
"

www.MySelfieNeedsNoFilter.com

SELF-LOVE
✤
PROPS

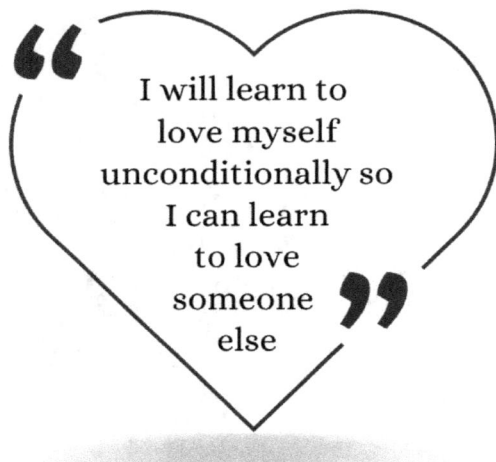

" I will learn to
love myself
unconditionally so
I can learn
to love
someone
else "

www.MySelfieNeedsNoFilter.com

SELF-LOVE
✣
PROPS

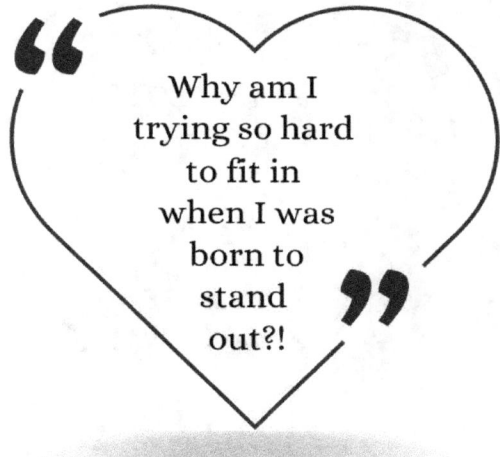

> Why am I
> trying so hard
> to fit in
> when I was
> born to
> stand
> out?!

www.MySelfieNeedsNoFilter.com

SELF-LOVE
PROPS

> I am the CEO of
> my life. I
> HIRE
> FIRE
> and
> PROMOTE
> accordingly.

www.MySelfieNeedsNoFilter.com

SELF-LOVE
✙
PROPS

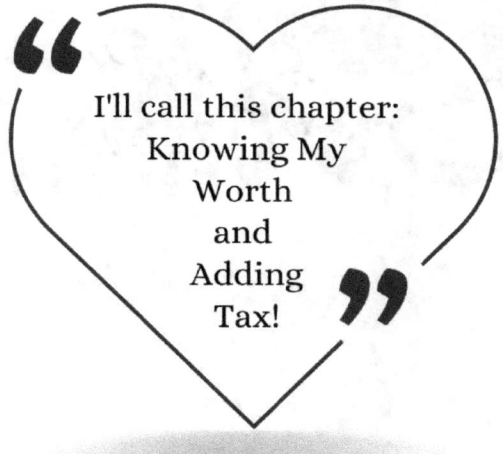

I'll call this chapter:
Knowing My
Worth
and
Adding
Tax!

www.MySelfieNeedsNoFilter.com

My Selfie NEEDS NO FILTER

Chapter Seven
Time to Upload

A happy ending typically occurs at the end of a story, where everything turns out for the best for the main character. The story may have taken you on an emotional rollercoaster of twists and turns, ups and downs, laughter and sadness. Even though some chapters may have been challenging for the main character, they didn't give up.

As the main character of your life's story, don't allow challenging chapters to hold you back from achieving your happy ending. It's just a few bad chapters, not your entire story. Embrace all your life's chapters, even the cringy and embarrassing ones. Those chapters make your life story an exciting book to read.

I want you to know that you deserve all the beautiful things that are currently happening in your life; and those that are soon to come. You are destined for greatness in a life full of happiness, excitement, and wonderment. Self-esteem, self-confidence, self-respect, self-care, and self-love are necessary components that create beauty within you. When all your selfie evels are balanced, get ready to upload.

When you upload your physical selfies, you transfer your pictures from your phone to another location. Likewise, when you upload your internal selfies, you transfer them from low to high levels, resulting in personal growth and leveling up.

Understanding how to take BeYOUtiful internal selfies to inspire a more confident YOU will ensure that your happy ending will last until the day after forever. Your future is bright, and you have many amazing things to look forward to. Remembering the valuable things this book provides will help you become a better leader and role model for everyone around you.

Leadership is a privilege that you should take very seriously. Making smart decisions, being kind, and supporting others are the traits of a great leader. Leadership starts with having the confidence in yourself to do incredible things. You're now equipped with the knowledge, skills, and resources to positively impact your community and the world.

This book has given you the secret sauce of competence, confidence, and compassion to find your lane and step into it! When you need a reminder, return to your favorite sections and allow them to inspire you. You have what it takes to accomplish all your goals and dreams. All you have to do is remember to tell yourself, "My selfie needs no filter. I'm BeYOUtiful as I am."

My Selfie
NEEDS NO FILTER

Chapter Eight
Power On

My Selfie Needs No Filter is an international anthem of empowerment and self-discovery for young ladies worldwide! This movement is for them to understand the importance of taking BeYOUtiful internal selfies and loving themselves from the inside out.

To kick off the movement, the 2022 First Annual **My Selfie Needs No Filter**: Little Ladies of Leadership Conference took place in Pensacola, Florida, known for its beautiful sugar-white sand beaches! This unforgettable experience had over 400 participants who traveled from Missouri, Texas, Louisiana, Mississippi, Alabama, Florida, and Georgia to attend this explosive event! Dynamic speakers, show-stopping performances, 360 Selfie Booths, fun games, door prizes, affordable vendors, free food, and much more were available for all in attendance!

The young ladies were asked the following three questions during the event and instructed to place their answers on the **My Selfie Needs No Filter** website:

1. What does the phrase, "**My Selfie Needs No Filter**", mean to you?
2. What was your favorite part of the conference?
3. What is your personal message regarding the conference?

Here's what a few of them had to say:

Kennede T. (17 yrs old)

- To me, My Selfie Needs No Filter means that my self-love, self-respect, and self-esteem don't need to be altered to fit the needs of others. You don't need to act a certain way to please someone else because if they don't like you, there is nothing you can do to make them like you; they will always have something to nitpick about.

- My favorite part of the conference was hearing everyone's stories and how the phrase "My selfie needs no filter" relates to them. I also enjoyed speaking on stage about my personal experiences with bullying and overcoming that.

- My message is, don't let filters fool you; behind the filter is a broken screen.

Jamoria N. (18yrs old)

- It means no matter what people can say about me, I'm still the most beautiful person in my eyes. No one can break me down. Also, I think it means whatever mountain that's in my way... God can move it out of the way, so I don't need a filter to hide my salvation.

- My favorite part was when we all got up and danced. It really brought joy to my heart.

- My message is the only person that can change you is YOU. Once you know you're OK, you won't let anybody steal your confidence because you fought hard for it. So be you & don't let others determine you.

Ollie T. (14yrs old)

- The meaning of My Selfie Needs No Filter changed significantly after meeting all of the beautiful people at the conference. Before the conference, it meant being happy and confident about my appearance. However, after the conference, I know it has an even deeper meaning than our outer appearance. My Selfie Needs No Filter means standing part of who I am both on the outside and inside. It means I do not need to change anything to make others happy. I am me! I am strong! I am unique! I am powerful! I am NOT ALONE!

- My favorite part of the conference was the feeling in the room as people could share their stories. I also loved being able to experience this with my mom. She made me very proud because she helped set up the conference. I know she brought me there because she believes in me and the change I can make. Being there with my mom made us even stronger together!

- My message is, thank you for a great day!

Anonymous (18yrs old)

- It means you don't have to change who you are or what you wear to fit in or look a certain way for people to think you are beautiful. God made all of his people beautiful in their image. As long as you believe, your light will forever shine, and you will continue to glow beyond anything you could ever imagine. That's what makes you beautiful.

- My favorite part of the conference was the dancing and the speakers who spoke.

- My message is I really enjoyed this, and it made me realize no matter how people may look at me, I'm beautiful in all aspects, and nobody can tell me differently now.

Anonymous (13yrs old)

- It means you're gorgeous, and don't let anybody

bring you down.

- My favorite part was when we did the model part.

- My message is, don't be insecure.

Anonymous (15yrs old)

- It means you don't need to change yourself for others.

- My favorite part was when everyone was dancing.

- My message is never to change yourself for others.

Ailani S. (11yrs old)

- It means being my authentic self and learning to love myself!

- My favorite part was feeling a sense of belonging and enjoying other girls my age. It was very relatable.

- My message is I enjoyed this conference. It gave me a true sense of understanding and zeal to continue being my best version.

Zamylah D. (13yrs old)

- It means, I'm me, I'm beautiful, I'm loved, I have confidence, and I believe in everything I do. No matter what anyone thinks, I know who I am and am beautiful inside and out.

- My favorite part was hearing all the positive and motivational speeches. The teen panel and everything they said. The runway fashion show and engaging with the audience. All the performances.

- I was once bullied and suicidal. I didn't want to live anymore because of what others said about me. I suffer from depression and anxiety, and I'm learning how to control my attacks. I'm so thankful for my mother and family because they help me get through one of the darkest moments in my life. Now I have my confidence back and self-esteem back. I'm happy; I know I'm loved. I'm surrounded by people who want to see me succeed and want the best for me. I overcame a lot at a young age.

Gabrielle B. (18yrs old)

- I take the phrase literally and figuratively. My literal selfies need no filter; skin has texture, and there's no shame in that. Figuratively, I do not need to cover up, blur, or edit who I am. I can be me automatically.

- My favorite part was when we all went to the center of the room, danced together, and hyped each other up.

- My message is every woman is worthy and valuable.

Aaliyah J. (14yrs old)

- It means being a leader, making good choices, and loving God.

- My favorite part was the activities and speakers.

- My message is I truly enjoyed the conference, and I love to praise dance.

Anonymous (14yrs old)

- To me, it means I don't need to change myself to fit in with other people.

- My favorite part was when Ms. Erica Lanes talked about the girl and her class.

- My favorite part was when Ms. Aleitha talked about what she went through because I am currently going through the same thing. I get called a stud/lesbian all the time.

Anonymous (28yrs old)

- It means being confident in your skin without worrying about what others feel about you and being able to walk around without being insecure about yourself.

- My favorite part was Mrs. Erica Lanes getting up

on stage with her student and speaking about bullying and Dr. Gaston telling us about being gritty
and staying gritty with encouraging words.

- I'm 28, and the words of encouragement you all
gave to the youth not only encouraged them but
also encouraged me to be confident in myself &
love myself rather than looking for it in someone
else.

To attend the next **My Selfie Needs No Filter**: Little Ladies of Leadership Conference, learn more about other exciting upcoming events, new book releases, and to purchase BeYOUtiful merchandise visit www.**MySelfieNeedsNoFilter**.com.

About the Author

Erica Lanes

Erica Lanes is considered a Florida girl with Mississippi melanin! She grew up on the Gulf Coast of the United States, where her family roots are planted in Mississippi, and her upbringing was grown in Florida. Her life's journey has also taken her from the Pacific Coast to the Atlantic Coast and across seas to Germany. A tragic head-on collision in 2015 left her wheelchair-bound, resulting in a life-long right leg limp. Perseverance, determination, and faith pulled her through her tribulations. She is now the CEO and President of Erica Lanes, LLC, and serves as a Leadership Specialist, Professional Speaker, and the author of **"My Selfie Needs No Filter"**.

Erica has served in many leadership positions and won several national, state, and local awards. She has been featured in several magazines and newspapers and has made guest appearances for news outlets such as CNN and local television and radio. Her most rewarding and unforgettable experience was serving as an 8th-grade middle school teacher while pursuing her Master's Degree in Healthcare Administration. She currently interacts with teens in her community and county school district, teaching them leadership, social, and life skills. In her spare time, Erica enjoys lying on the beach, listening to music, writing, reading books, and traveling with her husband, of 17 years and their two boys. You can visit her online at **www.EricaLanes.com.**

References

Ava, Amy. Mindful. (2018 May 23) Five Ways to Help Teens Build a Sense of Self-Worth. Retrieved from https://www.mindful.org/five-ways-to-help-teens-build-a-sense-of-self-worth/

Chang, Rachel. Biography.com (2021 Jan. 8) Aretha Franklin: The Powerful Meaning Behind Her Equality Anthem "Respect." Retrieve from https://www.biography.com/musicians/aretha-franklin-respect-meaning

Forgeard, Valerie. Brilliantio.com. (2022 Aug. 2). Why respect is important. Retrieved from https://brilliantio.com/why-respect-is-important/

JW.org. (n.d.) Young People Ask: How Can I Resist Peer Pressure to Have Sex? Retrieved from https://www.jw.org/en/bible-teachings/teenagers/ask/resist-peer-pressure-sex/

Merriam-Webster. (n.d.). Self-care. Merriam-Webster.com dictionary. Retrieved from https://www.merriam-webster.com/dictionary/self-care

Merriam-Webster. (n.d.). Self-confidence. Merriam-Webster.com dictionary. Retrieved from https://www.merriam-webster.com/dictionary/self-confidence

Merriam-Webster. (n.d.). Self-esteem. Merriam-Webster.com dictionary. Retrieved from https://www.merriam-webster.com/dictionary/self-esteem

Merriam-Webster. (n.d.). Self-love. Merriam-Webster.com dictionary. Retrieved from https://www.merriam-webster.com/dictionary/self-love

Merriam-Webster. (n.d.). Self-respect. Merriam-Webster.com dictionary. Retrieved from https://www.merriam-webster.com/dictionary/self-respect

Burke, Rose. The Minds Journal (n.d.). 8 Remarkable Psychological
        Benefits of Making Your Bed. Retrieved from https://theminds
        journal.com/psychological-benefits-of-making-your-bed/

N.H.S. (2020 Feb. 6) Raising Low Self-Esteem. Retrieved from
        https://www.nhs.uk/mental-health/self-help/tips-and-support
        /raise-low-self-esteem/

R. Morgan Griffin. WebMD.com (2010 July 21). Teen Hygiene Tips.
        Retrieved from https://www.webmd.com/parenting/features/
        teen-hygiene

Therapist.com. (2022 Dec. 15) What is self-esteem, and how can I
        improve mine? Therapist.com. Retrieved from https://therapist.
        com/self-development/what-is-self-esteem/

VeryWellMind.com. (2022 Nov. 1). What Is Self-Respect? Retrieved
        from https://www.verywellmind.com/self-respect-importance-
        influences-and-strategies-for-improvement-6823525

www.ingramcontent.com/pod-product-compliance
Lightning Source LLC
Chambersburg PA
CBHW060534130626
46553CB00002B/749